The Truth About The Fed
By Parker Bono

Also By Parker Bono

The Stance To Lead

The Stance To Get Elected

*As always,
I dedicate this book to the American
people and those who fight and fought
for my rights.*

Contents

Introduction

The Truth About The Fed is a book written to expose what truly is the Federal Reserve. The book explains the history of the Federal Reserve. It shows who truly benefits from the system, and it explains in depth the system. The book also proposes alternatives to the Federal Reserve and reasons to end the Federal Reserve.

The book is written by the 13 year old, 8th grader, Parker Bono. Parker obtained a passion for politics in 2015, and began getting politically involved ever since. Parker has also written two other political books titled The Stance To Lead and The Stance To Get Elected. Overall, this book will help you obtain new knowledge on how our financial system works and how people profit from it. Parker hopes you enjoy the book.

Chapter One
The Creation

"The Federal Reserve system is nothing more than legalized counterfeit." -Ron Paul

On November 10, 1910, elite bankers and political leaders met at an island off the coast of Georgia called Jekyll Island to create a new financial system. That's right: the people who created the financial system for our government had nothing to do with the U.S. government. Some of these people consisted of Nelson Aldrich, Arthur Shelton, Dr. A. Piatt Andrew, J.P. Morgan, Henry P. Davison, Frank A. Vanderlip and Paul M. Warburg.

Of course, these people didn't want people to know what they met about, or even the fact that they met. They tried everything they could to hide it, but they couldn't. They tried blacking out the windows on their means of transportation, but it didn't work. Eventually when the meeting became public, they said they were "duck hunting", when they we're really creating the most complex system of legalized theft in U.S. history.

Chapter Two
The Owners

"If you want to make enemies, try to change
something." -Woodrow Wilson

Now, this may come as a shock to some, but it
isn't all that shocking. The same people who
created the Federal Reserve own it. The
Federal Reserve doesn't need permission from
any branch of government to do whatever they
want. This makes them an independent entity.

However, the Federal Reserve is much more
than an independent entity. The Federal
Reserve has owners, they are the banking
elite. The Federal Reserve is separated into 12
different banks, but they all tell the same story.
In New York for example, 53% of the Federal
Reserve bank of New York is owned by two
banks: Chase and Citibank. This gives these
two companies control of the Federal Reserve
bank of New York as they are the primary
owners.

However, at all Federal Reserve banks, one
thing is certain: the Federal Reserve isn't
federal. The Federal Reserve has

stockholders. No federal agency in the U.S. has any stockholders. A share of stock is a percentage of ownership of a corporation, so therefore the stockholders a corporation are the owners of a corporation. Therefore, the Federal Reserve is a private corporation, with owners. To quote the Federal Reserve's own website, "The stockholders of the bank (Federal Reserve) shall be entitled to receive an annual dividend of 6 percent."

Now, in the beginning of this whole scam, the stock in the Federal Reserve was given to the biggest banks in the world. I would assume these banks kept their shares, as we saw in New York, but due to merging of companies and buying of companies, we can't trace who owns the stock in the Federal Reserve. If we audited the Federal Reserve, we could see. However, all attempts of this have failed.

Chapter Three
Caring

"The Federal Reserve is answerable to no
one." - Ronald Reagan

Our society is made from an array of
institutions. There are political institutions, legal
institutions, religious institutions, and many
more. These institutions have great influence
on creating our views. However, of all the
institutions that exist in our country, the least
understood is our monetary system.

Most Americans don't know or care about how
our money is made or the devastating effects it
has on our country. In a country where our
society itself is money, you should care.

If you don't care, the debt will continue to rise
and the system will continue to enslave us. We
the people are the only thing that can stop the
system from expanding to a point in which we
can never recover.

Chapter Four
How It's Made

"I believe that banking institutions are more
dangerous to our liberties than standing
armies." -Thomas Jefferson

Economics is typically viewed as boring or
confusing. When people try to follow
economics, they are given loads of financial
information and challenging math. This
typically stops people from learning more about
how economics work. However, this complexity
is just a mask used to cover up how our
system actually works.

Believe it or not, it's fairly simple. You don't
need to look on any websites or other sources
to understand how the system works. All you
have to do is look no further than the Federal
Reserve themselves.

In 2011, the Federal Reserve released a
document titled Modern Money Mechanics.
This document explained the practice of money
creation that is used by banks in America,
including the Federal Reserve.

On the very first page, they explain it all. "The purpose of this booklet is to describe the basic process of money creation in a "fractional reserve" banking system."

What is a fractional reserve banking system you might ask? Well, a fractional reserve banking system is a banking system in which banks do not have to keep all of the money you deposit. As a matter of fact, almost always banks must only keep a mere 10% of deposits in the banks. To quote the Federal Reserve, "Under current regulations, the reserve requirement against most transaction accounts is 10%." The rest of the money deposited can be lent out to others, deposited, lent out to others, and so on. In the end, a $100 deposit can create $1,000, out of thin air.

Now is when things start to get crazy. When the United States government wants money, the request that amount from the Federal Reserve. Let's say they request $10 billion. The Federal Reserve then will buy $10 billion in government bonds in exchange for that $10 billion. The government will then issue $10 billion worth of treasury bonds and will trade them with the Federal Reserve in exchange for

$10 billion. Treasury bonds are, to say simply, fancy pieces of paper that are supposedly worth a certain amount of money. Federal Reserve notes are nothing more than fancy pieces of paper as well. Once the government has their money, they will deposit the money into a bank and thus they create money. This of course was a generalization as this would most likely take place electronically with no paper being used at all. As a matter of fact, a mere 3% of the money supply exists physically. The other 97% exists in computers.

Now, logic would tell you that there has been $10 billion added to the money supply, right? Well, not quite. Whenever that $10 billion is deposited into a bank account, that money becomes part of the bank's reserves, just like any other deposit. Remember, the fractional reserve rate is 10%. This means that 10%, or $1 billion of the deposit is held while the other 90%, or $9 billion is considered an excessive reserve and can be used by the bank to issue loans.

Again , it would be logical to assume that that $9 billion is coming directly from the $10 billion, but this is not the case. What actually happens is that the $9 billion is simply created out of thin air on top of the $10 billion deposit. This is how the money supply expands. Again, to quote Modern Money Mechanics, "Of course, they (the banks) do not really pay out loans from the money they receive as deposits. If they did this, no additional money would be created. What they do when they make loans is to accept promissory notes (loan contracts) in exchange for credits (money) to the borrower's transaction account." To say it more simply, the $9 billion can be created out of thin air because there is a demand for loans and there is a $10 billion deposit to satisfy the reserve requirements.

Now, let's just say you or I go into this bank and borrows the $9 billion. They will then, most likely, take the money and either deposit it in their bank account or use the money to buy something, in which case the seller would take the money and put it in their bank account. This process would repeat and repeat until that $10 billion creates a total of $100 billion in new money, from thin air. In other words, for every deposit that is made into a bank, about 10 times that amount can be created from nothing.

Chapter Five
Inflation

"None are more hopelessly enslaved than those who falsely believe they are free."
-Johann Wolfgang

Now that you understand how money is created through the "fractional reserve" banking system, you might be wondering: what gives the new money value? The answer is the money that already exists. The new money steals the value the existing money supply has since the total amount of money is being increased disproportionately to the demand for goods and services that are bought with that money and as supply and demand catch up, prices rise, which brings down the purchasing power of each individual dollar. In other words, each dollar printed is worth less than the one before.

This is typically called inflation, and inflation is technically a hidden tax on we the people. One Tax that however is not hidden is the federal income tax, and this tax was created the same year as the Federal Reserve. Before the Federal Reserve existed, there was no IRS and no federal income tax. Our fractional reserve banking system is inflationary as since the act of expanding the money supply unproportionately will always devalue a currency.

Now, let me ask you something: for the most part, do you think people have the same things that they had in 1913? Absolutely. They had homes, cars, pets, and food. However, how much these things cost has changed extremely. $1 in 1913 requires requires $21.64 now to match value. This is a 95.37% devaluation of the dollar since the Federal Reserve was created. If a stock lost 95.37% of it's value, you probably wouldn't invest in it, would you?

Chapter Six
Debt

"A man in debt is so far a slave."
-Ralph Waldo Emerson

If what you have read so far seems insane, just wait. You will soon see that insanity is an understatement for the explanation of the Federal Reserve system.

In our financial system, debt is money, and money is debt. If you compared the charts of the U.S. money supply to the national debt, they would be practically the same. This is because of the fact that the more money there is out there, the more debt there is out there, and the more debt there is out there, the more money there is out there.

To put it differently, every single dollar in your wallet and in my wallet is owed to somebody. This is because the only way money can be created is through loans. This means that if ever single entity payed off their debt, there would be no money in existence. This does not include my plan as my plan involves selling, and making money from entities worldwide.

To quote the Federal Reserve, "If there were no debts in our money system, there wouldn't be any money." If the U.S. Treasury had the authority to issue money, this wouldn't be the case.

The only time in American history in which the national debt was payed off was in 1835 under President Andrew Jackson. One year before the debt was payed off, Andrew Jackson ended the national bank that preceded the Federal Reserve. This is not a coincidence. Andrew Jackson also warned us about what will happen if we reinstated a national bank.

To quote Andrew Jackson, "The bold efforts the present bank has made to control the government are but premonitions of the fate that awaits the American people should they be deluded into a perpetuation of this institution, or the establishment of another like it." Unfortunately, his message didn't last congress as 7 and a half decades after Jackson's presidency, congress and international bankers created the Federal Reserve and as long as it exists, debt is guaranteed.

Chapter Seven
Interest

"Give me control of a nation's money supply
and I care not who makes its laws."
-Amschel Rothschild

So far you have read about the reality that money is created out of debt, via loans. These loans are based on a bank's reserves, and through our fractional reserve system, any deposit can create 10 times the amount deposited, in the end devaluing the money supply, and raising prices.

But even after all of this, it still get's worse. I still have not showed you how interest fits into this.

When the government borrows money from the Federal Reserve, or when you or I borrow money from a bank, it must be payed back with interest. In other words, every single dollar in existence must be eventually returned to a bank, with interest paid as well. This is because the only way to create money is through banks.

But, if all money is borrowed from the Federal Reserve, and later is expanded by commercial banks, only something called the principal is being created in the money supply.

Now, you may be wondering where all the money is to cover the interest. The answer is... nowhere, it doesn't exist, it never can exist in our current system and never will exist in our current system. This means that the amount of money owed to the banks will always be more than the amount of money in circulation. This is why inflation is constantly occurring. New money is always needed to cover the debt built into the system that is caused by the need to pay back interest.

Our whole system transfers our wealth to the banks. If you are unable to pay your mortgage, they will take your property. This can make you mad when you realize that not only is a default inevitable due to our fractional reserve banking system, but also because of the fact that the money that was loaned to you from the bank didn't even legally exist to begin with.

Back in 1969 there was a court case on this exact issue. A man named Jerome challenged the foreclosure of his home by the bank. His argument in the case was that "the mortgage contract required both parties (him and the bank) each put up a legitimate form of property in the exchange." Jerome explained that the money wasn't the bank's property since it was created out of nothing whenever the loan was signed.

Do your remember what Modern Money Mechanics stated about loans? It said "What they do when they make loans is to accept promissory notes in exchange for credits." It also states "Reserves are unchanged by the loan transactions. But the deposit credits constitute new additions to the total deposits of the banking system." In other words, the money doesn't come out of the bank's existing assets. The bank merely invents it, putting up nothing of it's own except for supposed liability on paper.

During the trial, the bank's President, Mr. Morgan spoke. The judge's own note state "The bank's President admitted that in combination with the Federal Reserve Bank, they did create the money and credit upon it's books by bookkeeping entry. The money and credit first came into existence when they created it. Mr. Morgan admitted that no U.S. law or statute existed which gave him the right to do this. A lawful consideration must exist and be tendered to support the note. The Jury found that there was no lawful consideration and I agree. Only god can create something of value out of nothing." Due to this, Jerome kept his home. The result of this case is huge since every time someone borrows money from a bank, whether it's a mortgage loan or a credit card charge, the money given isn't just counterfeit, it is an illegitimate form of payment, and ultimately voids the contract, since the bank never had the money as property to begin with. Unfortunately, most people don't know about this, and the system will continue.

Chapter Eight
Slavery

"Well, I don't know as I want a lawyer to tell me what I cannot do. I hire him to tell how to do what I want to do." -J.P. Morgan

---

The ultimate question that you should ask from reading this book is: why? During the civil war, President Abraham Lincoln ignored the high interest loans that were offered by European banks. Instead, Lincoln decided to do what the founding fathers fought for: he created an independent and debt free currency. It was called the greenback.

Shortly after Lincoln did this, a document came to surface that circulated between British and American banking interests. The document stated "Slavery is but the owning of labor, and carries with it the care of laborers, while the European plan is that capital shall control labor by controlling wages. This can be done by controlling the money. It will not due to allow the greenback, as we can not control that."

The fractional reserve system, created by the federal reserve, which has spread to the majority of banks in the world is in fact a form of slavery. Think about it. Money is created out of debt, and what do people do when they are in debt? They will submit to employment to pay it off. But if money can only be made from the issue of loans, how can we ever have a debt free society? It can't, and that's exactly why the system was created.

It is the fear of losing assets along with the struggle to keep up with the pace of debt and inflation in the system, along with the scarcity of the money supply, that was created by the interest that can never be repaid. That is what keeps we the slaves in line. We, along with millions of other Americans, are running on a hamster wheel that powers the banking elite, since in the end of the day, who are you really working for? The banks. Money is created within banks and will end back into a bank. They are the true masters of our society, and we the people. Physical slavery requires people be fed and housed. Economic slavery intimidates people to feed and house themselves. It isn't bad to feed or house yourself, it is bad that it is done out of fear. This system is the greatest scam in human history.

As most walk oblivious, the banks continue to get better at their scam.

Chapter Nine
Banks

"It is well enough that people of the nation do not understand our banking and monetary system, for if they did, I believe there would be a revolution before tomorrow morning."
-Henry Ford

Before I tell you about the banks in the U.S., let me give you a little background on the dollar and explain to you why the dollar still survives.

In 1945, the Bretton Woods agreement made the dollar become the world's reserve currency. This meant that international products were priced in dollars. The agreement, which made the dollar the most powerful currency, was made under one condition: those dollars would be redeemable for gold at a rate of $35 per ounce. The U.S. promised they wouldn't print too much money, or cause too much inflation, but the Federal Reserve was only asked to do this. They weren't forced to do this, and they didn't do this.

During the Vietnam War, other countries realized that the U.S. was printing much more than they had in gold due to the fact that they were spending so much on the war. In response, other countries began asking for their gold. This caused the value of the dollar to plummet. This situation peaked in 1971 when France tried to withdraw their gold, but President Nixon refused to give it. On August 15, 1971, he announced he would stop allowing people to get gold for their dollars. To the other countries who had invested in the U.S., this was theft.

In 1973, President Nixon asked Saudi Arabia to only use U.S. dollars as payment for oil and to invest any profits into U.S. Treasury bonds. In return for this, Nixon offered military protection of Saudi Arabia's oil fields. The same offer was given to all countries in OPEC, and by 1975, all members of OPEC agreed to only sell oil in dollars. Moving the dollar away from gold and tieing it to oil forced all the countries in OPEC to maintain a large supply of Federal Reserve notes, or dollars and in order to get that paper, they would need to give the U.S. oil. This created something called the petrodollar. Paper was exported and oil was imported. It worked, and was the second

largest financial scam in history, behind the
Federal Reserve.

Now, onto the banks. Banks make a profit by
loaning out your money. Large banks are
typically known as too big to fail. Now, we don't
want banks to be too big to fail, but we don't
want to achieve this through regulation either.

Dodd-Frank should cease to exist, and before I
tell you why, let me give you a little history on
it. After the 2008 crisis, a bunch of Democratic
congressmen formed a bunch of banking
regulations that amounted to over 30,000
pages, which is almost as bad as our tax code.
Now, this new law didn't do what it was
supposed to. Because of Dodd-Frank, small
banks failed and big banks prospered. The
same rules apply to small banks and big
banks, and very few small banks are able to
survive because of this. Big banks are too big
to fail and big banks will never fail if they
maintain control over our monetary system.
Finally, Dodd-Frank probably won't succeed in
it's main goal to stop another financial crisis.
Mark my words: we are in a financial crisis. It
has already started and nobody, especially not
30,000 pages of regulations, can stop it.

Now, with all that being said, reform is necessary in the banking industry. I am a free market person but some changes just must be made after Dodd-Frank is repealed. I have a six point plan on how to fix the banks, and here it is.

The first thing that must be done to fix the banks is to raise the reserve requirements that banks must hold. As a matter of fact, these reserve requirements should be 100%. It may seem simple but banks should have to keep the money that you deposit in their vault. Most don't even know that this isn't currently how it works, but sadly it is. If we had 100% reserve rates, our money would be safe.

The second thing we must do is ensure that banks use their own money for their gambling purposes. When you or I gamble in Vegas, we need to use our money to fund it. Now, this is different for the banks. Banks use FDIC insured deposits to fund the risks they make, and if they don't succeed there, they call the Federal Reserve. Nobody in the world can pay themselves billions of dollars to take infinite amounts of risk with no money down, except banks.

The third thing I will do is change the tax code. This tax code, which would be a 10% flat tax for those above the poverty line, with no deductions, would help support long term investment. People need to realize that investing long term is the best way to get rich, and to help develop companies. There is no better way to give people the opportunity to do this than to give them more of their own money.

Fourthly, we will end too big to fail banks. We'll start with Goldman Sachs. This of course will be a side effect rather than a policy but it is essential. The government will never, never, never pay another penny to a bank. If they are going to fail, then they will fail. They also will no longer make our money, or be able to increase the money supply through inflation, as we will have 100% reserve rates. These banks have created a derivative market valued at over $700 Trillion. This is equal to more than 10 times the GDP of the world. We don't know much about these derivatives as the banks keep it secret. For instance, Citibank has assets that amount to about $2 trillion yet they have derivatives that amount to over $54 trillion. If a bank is going to fall, we will let it but we won't let it bring down our economy with.

The next thing that must be done is to end the issuing of U.S. Treasury Bonds. These Treasury bonds are our debt, and the reason the Federal Reserve can charge us extra money. These bonds are impossible to pay off without going into debt. If we didn't issue any more Treasury bonds, within 6 years, 90% of current bonds would mature and within 30 years, Treasury bonds would cease to exist. This would only be beneficial to the U.S. as no longer would we have debt from these bonds and the U.S. government wouldn't function any differently. They would only spend less on bonds, and eventually nothing.

Finally, we must enact true transparency. We must expose the banks like we will with the Federal Reserve, via audit, prior to ending it. Now, people are going to fight me, and that's OK. These people don't want the scheme to end, and they don't want people to understand the scheme, but I will make sure they do. I will show Americans that the whole system is a taxpayer subsidized form of theft that makes the bankers rich. Taxpayers pay billions each year to the banks. They run a $700 trillion scam. The U.S. can't let it continue this way.

Chapter Ten
The Constitutionality

"The inability of the colonists to get power to issue their own money permanently out of the hands of George III and the international bankers was the prime reason for the Revolutionary War." -Benjamin Franklin

---

Not only is our whole monetary system wrong: it is also unconstitutional. The colonists knew the danger of a monetary system in which central banks could just print up pieces of paper, and fought against it. Therefore, the founding father put into the constitution "No State shall make any Thing but gold and silver Coin a Tender in Payment of Debts." Until Nixon, you used to be able to go and redeem your pieces of paper in exchange for gold, but now you are stuck with useless pieces of paper with writing on them that are owed back to the banks with interest that ultimately enslave you to pay the banks. Also, the Constitution gives the federal government 30 powers and states all other powers are given to the states. None of the powers granted to the federal

government include the formation of a central
bank.

Thomas Jefferson fought against Alexander
Hamilton in the formation of a central bank.
The bankers however won. Shortly after, that
central bank crumbled. A new one popped up
and it crumbled because of Andrew Jackson.
Killing the bank was one of Jackson's greatest
accomplishments. A little under a century later,
the Federal Reserve was created and
Americans have been stuck with it ever since.
It caused the Great Depression, it has caused
the dollar to lose over 95% of it's value, and it
will also cause the next Great Depression. The
founding fathers must be so disappointed in
what our banking system is today.

Chapter Eleven
End The Fed

"A society that puts equality before freedom will get neither. A society that puts freedom before equality will get a high degree of both."

I have 10 reasons why I believe we should end the Federal Reserve, and I will explain them to you right now. If we would like true economic prosperity, we must abolish the monopoly known as the Federal Reserve.

The first reason for abolition is the simple fact that the Federal Reserve, and the banks that own it, have far too much power over our economy. Our central bank has total power and control of the money supply. They can create however much money they want since it isn't backed by anything and they can do so with no consequences whatsoever. This could be in the form of a shortage or an increase of the money supply. The result would be deflation or inflation, both of which are bad and are taxes on we the people. The founding fathers would be outraged if they knew that a

central bank had the power to, without
restriction, control our economy as a whole.
The second reason we must end the Federal
Reserve is because the Federal Reserve has
devalued the dollar. It has caused the dollar to
go down in value over 95%. As I said earlier, it
now takes $24.61 to back up one dollar from
1913. This is an over 95% devaluation. We
have a thing called supply and demand, and
when the Federal Reserve mass produces
money not proportional to inflation rates, the
value of the dollar goes down. Every dollar
printed is worth less than the one before.
Unless we want our pieces of paper known as
dollars to be worth less than paper, we must
end the Federal Reserve

Reason three for ending the Federal Reserve
is because the hidden tax known as inflation
hurts middle class and poor Americans the
most. The fact we have high inflation rates is
enough reason to end the Federal Reserve,
but one thing most don't know is that this tax
hurts poor and middle class Americans more
than any other group. Inflation is not the rise of
prices, this is a result of inflation. Inflation is the
increase of the money supply. Inflation hurts
those with lower incomes more since they have

less money to spare. Now their money's worth less and so is their work and time.

The fourth reason we must end the Federal Reserve is because of the fact that the Federal Reserve is run and owned by unelected officials. The owners of the Federal Reserve are private banks and those who "run" the Federal Reserve are an elected. They are called the Board of Governors. This makes those who run the Federal Reserve unaccountable to we the people. The Board of Governors decide the purchasing power and price of our money while the banks and their owners make profits from the whole system.

The fifth reason to end the Federal Reserve is because of the fact that it has destabilized our economy as a whole. The Federal Reserve has caused our economy do go on an up and down roller coaster. The economy of our country was far more stable before the implementation of the Federal Reserve than it was after it. There is a theory that explains all of our booms and busts in our economy called the Australian Business Cycle Theory. The theory says that a fake "boom" will happen when the Federal Reserve lowers interest rates, which increases the money supply. The losses from this are worse than the gains. This expansion of money can't last forever, which means loss is ensured. Reason six for ending the Federal Reserve is the most interesting one. Reason six for ending the Federal Reserve is the amount of secrecy behind the organization. Our central bank has no transparency whatsoever. The Federal Reserve has never been fully audited by anyone or thing. The Federal Reserve claims that an audit to it's monopoly would hurt what they call their "independence". This wouldn't be a result of an audit, and as a matter of fact, an audit would expose what the Federal Reserve has been doing for over a century.

The seventh reason to abolish the monopoly is the fact that the Federal Reserve benefits special interest groups and elite at the expense of we the people. While most fall, others jump. In 2008, some people benefited dramatically. The Federal Reserve benefits the special interest groups and big bankers as they get access to the money before inflation occurs and devalues the money. This is the main reason why lobbyists fight so hard against change made to the Federal Reserve. Bankers also profit from this as they make profits on our money from the fractional reserve system. Any change to the system would hurt them, so they rally to maintain the system.

Reason number eight to end the Federal Reserve is something I told you about earlier. The Federal Reserve is unconstitutional. Like I said earlier, gold and silver are the only means of money that should be allowed in the U.S. If we are going to use paper as our money, it at least should be backed by gold or silver. Also, the Constitution gives the federal government thirty enumerated powers. None of these powers is the right to create a central bank. This Constitution should be obeyed and the Federal Reserve should be ended.

The ninth reason to end the Federal Reserve is the fact that the Federal Reserve constantly bails out big banks. The Federal Reserve will help out their friends known as the international bankers at all costs. In 2011, due to a Freedom of Information Act request, the Federal Reserve had to release over 28,000 pages. These pages showed who recipients were of the Federal Reserve's money. In the crisis of 2008, the Federal Reserve's top recipients of funds were international banks. Some of these banks were Dexia SA, Depfa Bank Plc, the

Bank of China, and the Arab Banking Corp. To me, this is treason. Why is the Federal Reserve helping the Bank of China in a time of crisis? Treason, defined by the Constitution, is "levying war against the United States" or "adhering to their enemies, giving them aid or comfort." I think a stack of cash counts as aid, don't you?

Also, in 2011, the Federal Reserve was partially audited by the Government Accountability Office. However, the Government Accountability Office was not allowed to see market operations, discount window lending, or the Federal Reserve's transactions with foreign banks and governments. So basically, they couldn't see the important information. What they however did find out from this partial audit was that the Federal Reserve gave over $16 trillion in secret bailouts of banks and governments. All of this happened without one word said about it in Congress, since the Federal Reserve has no oversight. To quote former Federal Reserve chairman, Alan Greenspan, "The Federal Reserve is an independent entity, and that means basically that there is no other agency of government which can overrule actions that

we take." If this information came from just a
partial audit, imagine what will come out from a
full, real audit.

The tenth and final reason to end the Federal
Reserve is the fact that the Federal Reserve
promotes deficit spending. The government
can only get money through taxes or through
borrowing money from the Federal Reserve,
and even the money that they get from taxes
was put into circulation by borrowing money
from the Federal Reserve. The government
vastly prefers to borrow money rather than tax
due to public opinion. This method however is
the worst method. With this system, the
government can just borrow however much
printed money they want. The whole system is
a never ending cycle. The government borrows
money, which creates debt. The government
then uses some of this money to pay for what
they want, but they typically spend more than
they have, so that creates more debt, and next
time they want something, they will need more
money, and it never ends. The debt also
accumulates over time, as does interest.
Voters could elect people that will cut taxes all
they want, and lenders can also stop lending to
the U.S. government all they want as well,

because none of that matters. The number one lender, the Federal Reserve, still has an active printing press and the government has an active thirst for spending, AKA debt.

Chapter Twelve
Replace The Fed

"The real tragedy of the poor is the poverty of
their aspirations." -Adam Smith

Now, let's assume that we end the Federal
Reserve. The only thing left to do is replace the
system. I have 5 ideas as to what should
replace the Federal Reserve, but ultimately,
one of them is the best. Now, during the
transition, the economy may feel some
suffering, but ultimately, it will not be as bad as
it would have been if we continued the system
on the basis of hopeless hope. The dollar will
go to zero if we do nothing and debt will grow
even more than it does right now.

The first idea of replacement is simple. The
first idea for replacement is that we back our
money with gold and silver. We could either
issue new money backed by gold and silver, or
back every dollar currently in existence to an
amount of gold or silver. Gold and silver are
proven forms of safe currencies, and would
stabilize our economy. However, if we backed
every current dollar with an amount of gold or
silver, we couldn't print anymore.

The second possible replacement to the
Federal Reserve is a form of local currencies.
Local currencies are already legal in the U.S.
"as long as it does not look like dollars, as long
as denominations are at least $1.00 in value,
and if it's regarded as taxable income." So
basically, they are currencies tied to dollars
that aren't called dollars and are created at the
local level. Some communities have their own
currencies, and it is an overall good alternative
to a debt based system that the federal
government doesn't really need to worry about,
they will just receive tax dollars from people. If
we made this our new monetary system, the
constitution would be followed, as the federal
government doesn't have the right to create a
central bank, and the whole system would get
a whole lot simpler and debt free, at least for
the federal government.

A third potential replacement to the Federal
Reserve are credit unions and state banks.
North Dakota already adopted this policy, they
have a state bank, and it has worked out well
for them. We don't like the fractional reserve
system, but it is possible to take advantage of
the system for ourselves. We would do this by
replacing the Federal Reserve with credit

unions and state banks. These banks and credit unions only loan out their money to local projects or businesses, which help develop communities. The banks are also owned by the depositors, not banking elite. In North Dakota, they only make in state loans that came from deposits made by the state treasury, and in the end, all of the profits go back into the state and help develop communities. In this case scenario, the credit unions or state banks could use new money, as long as the currency has value and the currency is trusted by we the people.

The fourth possible alternative to the Federal Reserve is a form of U.S. Treasury issued currency. This is my favorite idea, and I would like for them to be backed by gold and silver. If the U.S. Treasury printed our money, they could do it debt free. We saw this happen in the 1800's with the Greenback, created under President Lincoln. This however wasn't the only time in U.S. history that we made debt free, Treasury issued currency. In colonial times, we did the same thing. Benjamin Franklin called it "honest money", and that's exactly what it was. To quote Benjamin Franklin, "In the Colonies we issue our own money. It is called Colonial Scrip. We issue it in proper proportion to make the products pass easily from the producers to the consumers. In this manner, creating ourselves our own paper money, we control its purchasing power, and we have no interest to pay to no one." Of course, if we made this the law, we would be opposed by practically every banker, as they would no longer profit from the system. This would also make the dollar useless, but it already inevitably will be. This system would save our country, especially if this new currency was backed by gold. Now, with that being said, we did have a President in recent times try to make this the law of the land. His name was John F. Kennedy. JFK attempted to end the Federal Reserve's ability to charge us interest and tried to make it so the Treasury issued our money. He also tried to make sure that this new money was backed by silver. He did this on June 4th, 1963 by signing executive order 11110. Less than 6 months later, he was killed in Dallas. Lyndon B. Johnson became President next, and he repealed executive order 11110. Like I said before, if we made this system our new law of the land, we could have debt free money that is stable.

The fifth and final potential replacement to the Federal Reserve is the formation of a bartering system. This system would seem like a setback hundreds of years, but it would be fair. I would trade you something you value for something I value. This system is the oldest form of trade in the world, and it would work, however, due to the fact that other developed countries don't use the system, it may not be the best thing for the U.S. as another country will be able to jump in and become the number one used form of currency.

Overall, the Federal Reserve must end, and it must be replaced. I believe that the best thing to replace the Federal Reserve with would be a Treasury issued currency backed by an amount of gold and silver as this system would be stable and debt free. I however would back almost any plausible proposals that ensure that the currency is debt free and the currency is stable, both of which we currently lack in our money. Only you can help end this monopoly, and being informed is the first step.

Index

A

E

F

Y

year, 5
York, 7-8
You, 10
you, 5, 7, 9-10